contents

The oven temperatures in this book are for conventional ovens; if you have a fan-forced oven, decrease the temperature by 10-20 degrees.

D0005181

classic
pizzas

In 1889, during a visit to Naples, Queen Margherita of Savoy was served a pizza resembling the colors of the Italian flag, red (tomato), white (mozzarella) and green (basil). This kind of pizza has been named after the Queen as Pizza Margherita.

margherita pizza

⅔ cup (170g) bottled tomato sauce
7½ ounces (240g) buffalo mozzarella cheese, sliced thinly
¼ cup loosely packed fresh small basil leaves

pizza dough
1½ cups (225g) bread flour or plain (all-purpose) flour
1 teaspoon (4g) dried yeast
1 teaspoon superfine sugar
1 teaspoon fine table salt
1 tablespoon olive oil
½ cup (125ml) warm water, approximately

1 Make pizza dough.
2 Preheat oven to 475°F. Oil two oven or pizza trays; place in heated oven.
3 Divide dough in half; roll each half on floured surface into a 12-inch round. Place on trays.
4 Spread pizza bases with sauce; top with cheese.
5 Bake pizzas about 15 minutes or until bases are browned and crisp. Serve sprinkled with basil.

pizza dough Combine flour, yeast, sugar and salt in medium bowl; make a well in the center. Stir in oil and enough of the water to mix to a soft dough. Knead dough on floured surface about 10 minutes or until smooth and elastic. Place dough in large oiled bowl, cover; stand in a warm place about 1 hour or until dough doubles in size. Turn dough onto floured surface; knead until smooth.

prep + cook time 30 minutes (+ standing) **serves** 4
nutritional count per serving 15g total fat (6.8g saturated fat); 358 cal; 38.1g carbohydrate; 16.4g protein; 2.8g fiber

We used buffalo mozzarella, but you can use any mozzarella, or the same amount of large bocconcini.

To make the classic quattro stagione (Italian for "four seasons") pizza, simply keep the olives, ham, mushrooms and artichokes on separate quarters of the pizza.

capricciosa pizza

⅔ cup (170g) bottled tomato sauce

1½ cups (150g) coarsely grated mozzarella cheese

2½ ounces (80g) shaved leg ham, chopped coarsely

2 ounces (60g) small button mushrooms, sliced thinly

4 ounces (130g) drained char-grilled artichokes, halved

⅓ cup (40g) pitted black olives

pizza dough

1½ cups (225g) bread flour or plain (all-purpose) flour

1 teaspoon (4g) dried yeast

1 teaspoon superfine sugar

1 teaspoon fine table salt

1 tablespoon olive oil

½ cup (125ml) warm water, approximately

1 Make pizza dough.

2 Preheat oven to 475°F. Oil two oven or pizza trays; place in heated oven.

3 Divide dough in half; roll each half on floured surface into a 12-inch round. Place on trays.

4 Spread pizza bases with sauce; top with cheese, ham, mushrooms, artichokes and olives.

5 Bake pizzas about 15 minutes or until bases are browned and crisp.

pizza dough Combine flour, yeast, sugar and salt in medium bowl; make a well in the center. Stir in oil and enough of the water to mix to a soft dough. Knead dough on floured surface about 10 minutes or until smooth and elastic. Place dough in large oiled bowl, cover; stand in a warm place about 1 hour or until dough doubles in size. Turn dough onto floured surface; knead until smooth.

prep + cook time 35 minutes (+ standing) **serves** 4
nutritional count per serving 15.1g total fat
(6.3g saturated fat); 391 cal; 41g carbohydrate;
20.8g protein; 4.1g fiber

garlicky mushroom pizza

½ ounce (10g) dried porcini mushrooms
2 tablespoons olive oil
1 clove garlic, crushed
7½ ounces (240g) buffalo mozzarella, sliced thinly
6½ ounces (200g) small button mushrooms,
    sliced thinly
1 tablespoon olive oil, extra
2 tablespoons coarsely chopped fresh
    flat-leaf parsley

pizza dough
1½ cups (225g) bread flour or plain (all-purpose)
    flour
1 teaspoon (4g) dried yeast
1 teaspoon superfine sugar
1 teaspoon fine table salt
1 tablespoon olive oil
½ cup (125ml) warm water, approximately

1 Make pizza dough.
2 Preheat oven to 475°F. Oil two rectangular oven trays or pizza trays; place in heated oven.
3 Place porcini mushrooms in small heatproof bowl, cover with boiling water; stand about 10 minutes or until soft, drain.
4 Meanwhile, divide dough in half; roll each half on floured surface into 8-inch x 12-inch rectangle. Place on trays.
5 Brush bases with combined oil and garlic. Top with cheese and both mushrooms, season; drizzle with extra oil.
6 Bake about 15 minutes or until bases are browned and crisp. Serve sprinkled with parsley.

pizza dough Combine flour, yeast, sugar and salt in medium bowl; make a well in the center. Stir in oil and enough of the water to mix to a soft dough. Knead dough on floured surface about 10 minutes or until smooth and elastic. Place dough in large oiled bowl, cover; stand in a warm place about 1 hour or until dough doubles in size. Turn dough onto floured surface; knead until smooth.

prep + cook time 35 minutes (+ standing) **serves** 4
nutritional count per serving 28.1g total fat (8.7g saturated fat); 471 cal; 35.7g carbohydrate; 17.6g protein; 3.3g fiber

Reserve porcini soaking liquid for use in risotto, pasta sauce or soups.

Quattro formaggi means 'four cheeses' in Italian; while any number of cheeses could be used, we have opted to use the more traditional cheeses in this recipe. Grana padano is a less expensive parmesan cheese than parmiggiano reggiano, but is just as good for cooking.

quattro formaggi pizza

3 ounces (100g) bocconcini cheese, sliced thinly
½ cup (40g) finely grated parmesan cheese
½ cup (50g) coarsely grated fontina cheese
1½ ounces (50g) gorgonzola cheese, crumbled

pizza dough
1½ cups (225g) bread flour or plain (all-purpose)
   flour
1 teaspoon (4g) dried yeast
1 teaspoon superfine sugar
1 teaspoon fine table salt
1 tablespoon olive oil
½ cup (125ml) warm water, approximately

1 Make pizza dough.
2 Preheat oven to 475°F. Oil two oven or pizza trays; place in heated oven.
3 Divide dough into four pieces; roll each piece on floured surface into 4-inch x 8-inch slipper shapes. Place on trays.
4 Top pizza bases with bocconcini; sprinkle with remaining cheeses.
5 Bake pizzas about 15 minutes or until bases are browned and crisp.

pizza dough Combine flour, yeast, sugar and salt in medium bowl; make a well in the center. Stir in oil and enough of the water to mix to a soft dough. Knead dough on floured surface about 10 minutes or until smooth and elastic. Place dough in large oiled bowl, cover; stand in a warm place about 1 hour or until dough doubles in size. Turn dough onto floured surface; knead until smooth.

prep + cook time 30 minutes (+ standing) **makes** 4
nutritional count per pizza 20.5g total fat (10.6g saturated fat); 404 cal; 34.9g carbohydrate; 19.2g protein; 1.8g fiber

Naples is widely credited as the birthplace of pizza, where it was originally sold to the city's poor by street vendors. The world's first pizzeria was opened there in 1830 and is still in operation today. The beauty of the napoletana pizza lies in its simplicity. Use only the best and freshest ingredients to achieve the most delicious authentic pizza.

napoletana pizza

⅔ cup (170g) bottled tomato sauce
2½ cups (250g) coarsely grated mozzarella cheese
½ cup (60g) pitted black olives
8 drained anchovy fillets, halved
2 teaspoons rinsed, drained capers
⅓ cup loosely packed fresh oregano leaves

pizza dough
1½ cups (225g) bread flour or plain (all-purpose) flour
1 teaspoon (4g) dried yeast
1 teaspoon superfine sugar
1 teaspoon fine table salt
1 tablespoon olive oil
½ cup (125ml) warm water, approximately

1 Make pizza dough.
2 Preheat oven to 475°F. Oil two oven or pizza trays; place in heated oven.
3 Divide dough in half; roll each half on floured surface into a 12-inch round. Place on trays.
4 Spread pizza bases with sauce; top with cheese, olives, anchovies, capers and oregano.
5 Bake pizzas about 15 minutes or until bases are browned and crisp.

pizza dough Combine flour, yeast, sugar and salt in medium bowl; make a well in the center. Stir in oil and enough of the water to mix to a soft dough. Knead dough on floured surface about 10 minutes or until smooth and elastic. Place dough in large oiled bowl, cover; stand in a warm place about 1 hour or until dough doubles in size. Turn dough onto floured surface; knead until smooth.

prep + cook time 30 minutes (+ standing) **serves** 4
nutritional count per serving 20.1g total fat (9.7g saturated fat); 451 cal; 41.5g carbohydrate; 24.5g protein; 3g fiber

potato and sausage pizza

2 tablespoons olive oil

2 cloves garlic, chopped finely

9½ ounces (300g) bocconcini cheese, sliced thinly

3 baby red-skinned potatoes (180g), unpeeled, sliced thinly

1 tablespoon fresh rosemary leaves

8 ounces (250g) spicy italian sausages

pizza dough

1½ cups (225g) bread flour or plain (all-purpose) flour

1 teaspoon (4g) dried yeast

1 teaspoon superfine sugar

1 teaspoon fine table salt

1 tablespoon olive oil

½ cup (125ml) warm water, approximately

1 Make pizza dough.

2 Preheat oven to 475°F. Oil two oven or pizza trays; place in heated oven.

3 Divide dough in half; roll each half on floured surface into 6-inch x 12-inch slipper shapes. Place on trays.

4 Brush half the oil over bases; sprinkle with half the garlic. Top with cheese then potato in a single layer. Brush with remaining oil; sprinkle with remaining garlic and rosemary, season. Squeeze sausage meat from casings; drop small pieces on pizzas.

5 Bake pizzas about 12 minutes or until bases are browned and crisp.

pizza dough Combine flour, yeast, sugar and salt in medium bowl; make a well in the center. Stir in oil and enough of the water to mix to a soft dough. Knead dough on floured surface about 10 minutes or until smooth and elastic. Place dough in large oiled bowl, cover; stand in a warm place about 1 hour or until dough doubles in size. Turn dough onto floured surface; knead until smooth.

prep + cook time 40 minutes (+ standing) **serves** 4
nutritional count per serving 39.6g total fat (15.2g saturated fat); 642 cal; 42.9g carbohydrate; 27g protein; 3.7g fiber

Use a mandoline or V-slicer to cut the potatoes into paper-thin slices.

calzone with pepperoni

⅓ cup (85g) bottled tomato sauce

6½ ounces (200g) bocconcini cheese, chopped coarsely

1½ ounces (50g) thinly sliced pepperoni

6 marinated artichoke hearts (75g), drained, halved

4 slices bottled roasted red bell pepper (170g), sliced thickly

¼ cup (30g) pitted black olives

¼ cup coarsely chopped fresh basil

1 teaspoon olive oil

pizza dough

2½ cups (375g) bread flour or plain (all-purpose) flour

2 teaspoons (7g) dried yeast

2 teaspoons superfine sugar

2 teaspoons fine table salt

2 tablespoons olive oil

1 cup (250ml) warm water, approximately

1 Make pizza dough.

2 Preheat oven to 475°F. Oil two oven or pizza trays; place in heated oven.

3 Divide dough in half; roll each half on floured surface into a 12-inch round.

4 Spread one half of both bases with sauce. Top with cheese, pepperoni, artichoke, red bell pepper, olives and basil; season. Brush edges with a little water; fold dough over filling, press edges to seal. Place calzones on trays; brush with oil.

5 Bake about 15 minutes or until calzones are browned and crisp.

pizza dough Combine flour, yeast, sugar and salt in medium bowl; make a well in the center. Stir in oil and enough of the water to mix to a soft dough. Knead dough on floured surface about 10 minutes or until smooth and elastic. Place dough in large oiled bowl, cover; stand in a warm place about 1 hour or until dough doubles in size. Turn dough onto floured surface; knead until smooth.

prep + cook time 30 minutes (+ standing) **serves** 4
nutritional count per serving 25.9g total fat (9.3g saturated fat); 674 cal; 78.7g carbohydrate; 27.3g protein; 7.7g fiber

eggplant, tomato and basil pizza

¼ cup (60ml) olive oil

1 medium eggplant (300g), unpeeled, sliced thinly

⅔ cup (170g) bottled tomato sauce

9½ ounces (300g) buffalo mozzarella, sliced thinly

6½ ounces (200g) cherry tomatoes

2 tablespoons fresh small basil leaves

1 teaspoon balsamic vinegar

pizza dough

1½ cups (225g) bread flour or plain (all-purpose) flour

1 teaspoon (4g) dried yeast

1 teaspoon superfine sugar

1 teaspoon fine table salt

1 tablespoon olive oil

½ cup (125ml) warm water, approximately

1 Make pizza dough.

2 Meanwhile, heat oil in large frying pan; cook eggplant, in batches, until browned lightly and tender. Drain on paper towels.

3 Preheat oven to 475°F. Oil two oven or pizza trays; place in heated oven.

4 Divide dough in half; roll each half on floured surface into a 12-inch round. Place on trays.

5 Spread pizza bases with sauce; top with cheese, eggplant and tomatoes. Season.

6 Bake pizzas about 15 minutes or until bases are browned and crisp. Serve sprinkled with basil, drizzle with vinegar.

pizza dough Combine flour, yeast, sugar and salt in medium bowl; make a well in the center. Stir in oil and enough of the water to mix to a soft dough. Knead dough on floured surface about 10 minutes or until smooth and elastic. Place dough in large oiled bowl, cover; stand in a warm place about 1 hour or until dough doubles in size. Turn dough onto floured surface; knead until smooth.

prep + cook time 40 minutes (+ standing) **serves** 4 **nutritional count per serving** 31.2g total fat (10.2g saturated fat); 534 cal; 41.2g carbohydrate; 20.1g protein; 5.3g fiber

We used buffalo mozzarella, but you can use the same amount of large bocconcini instead.

We used buffalo mozzarella but you can use the same amount of large bocconcini instead. This vegetarian pizza, also known as crudaiola, often uses arugula instead of basil.

fresh tomato pizza

⅔ cup (170g) bottled tomato sauce
8 ounces (250g) mixed tomatoes,
   chopped coarsely
4½ ounces (150g) buffalo mozzarella,
   sliced thinly
1 tablespoon olive oil
1 clove garlic, chopped finely
¼ cup loosely packed fresh small basil leaves
1 tablespoon pine nuts, roasted
¼ cup (20g) parmesan cheese

pizza dough
1½ cups (225g) bread flour or plain (all-purpose)
   flour
1 teaspoon (4g) dried yeast
1 teaspoon superfine sugar
1 teaspoon fine table salt
1 tablespoon olive oil
½ cup (125ml) warm water, approximately

1 Make pizza dough.
2 Preheat oven to 475°F. Oil two oven or pizza trays; place in heated oven.
3 Divide dough in half; roll each half on floured surface into 6-inch x 16-inch slipper shapes. Place on trays.
4 Spread pizza bases with sauce. Bake about 15 minutes or until bases are browned and crisp.
5 Top pizzas with tomato and mozzarella, drizzle with oil; season. Sprinkle with garlic, basil, nuts and parmesan.

pizza dough Combine flour, yeast, sugar and salt in medium bowl; make a well in the center. Stir in oil and enough of the water to mix to a soft dough. Knead dough on floured surface about 10 minutes or until smooth and elastic. Place dough in large oiled bowl, cover; stand in a warm place about 1 hour or until dough doubles in size. Turn dough onto floured surface; knead until smooth.

prep + cook time 35 minutes (+ standing) **serves** 4
nutritional count per serving 20.3g total fat (6.4g saturated fat); 411 cal; 39.7g carbohydrate; 15.3g protein; 4.1g fiber

seafood pizza

16 small black mussels (225g)
1 cup (250ml) water
⅔ cup (170g) bottled tomato sauce
2 tablespoons olive oil
12 uncooked medium shrimp (350g)
2 cloves garlic, sliced thinly
6½ ounces (200g) baby octopus, cleaned, quartered
3½ ounces (100g) cherry tomatoes
1 dried long red chili, sliced thinly
1 tablespoon fresh dill
1 tablespoon fresh flat-leaf parsley leaves

pizza dough

1½ cups (225g) bread flour or plain (all-purpose) flour
1 teaspoon (4g) dried yeast
1 teaspoon superfine sugar
1 teaspoon fine table salt
1 tablespoon olive oil
½ cup (125ml) warm water, approximately

1 Make pizza dough.
2 Combine mussels and the water in medium saucepan; cook, covered, about 1 minute or until shells open. Drain mussels; leave on the half-shell.
3 Meanwhile, preheat oven to 475°F. Oil two oven or pizza trays; place in heated oven.
4 Divide dough in half; roll each half on floured surface into a 12-inch round. Place on trays.
5 Spread pizza bases with sauce; drizzle with half the oil. Bake about 6 minutes or until base is browned lightly.
6 Meanwhile, shell and devein shrimp.
7 Top pizzas with garlic, seafood, tomatoes and chili; season. Drizzle with remaining oil. Bake about 5 minutes or until bases are browned and crisp and seafood is cooked. Serve sprinkled with herbs.

pizza dough Combine flour, yeast, sugar and salt in medium bowl; make a well in the center. Stir in oil and enough of the water to mix to a soft dough. Knead dough on floured surface about 10 minutes or until smooth and elastic. Place dough in large oiled bowl, cover; stand in a warm place about 1 hour or until dough doubles in size. Turn dough onto floured surface; knead until smooth.

prep + cook time 50 minutes (+ standing) **serves** 4
nutritional count per serving 16.4g total fat (2.4g saturated fat); 432 cal; 39.9g carbohydrate; 29.3g protein; 3.6g fiber

pizzettas
& party pizzas

Prosciutto, a thinly-sliced Italian, dry-cured ham, comes in two varieties: prosciutto crudo (raw) and prosciutto cotto (cooked). Here we have used prosciutto crudo.

pesto, bocconcini and prosciutto pizzettas

12-inch round pizza base (220g)
1½ tablespoons basil pesto
8 cherry bocconcini cheeses (120g), each cut
    into 3 slices
1½ ounces (45g) thinly sliced prosciutto,
    torn coarsely
24 fresh small basil leaves

1 Preheat oven to 475°F. Oil two oven trays; place in heated oven.
2 Cut 24 2-inch rounds from pizza base; spread rounds with pesto. Place rounds on trays.
3 Bake pizzettas about 5 minutes or until browned and crisp.
4 Serve topped with prosciutto, cheese and basil.

prep + cook time 20 minutes **makes** 24
nutritional count per pizzetta 1.7g total fat (0.7g saturated fat); 44 cal; 4.9g carbohydrate; 2.1g protein; 0.4g fiber

lamb, potato and feta party pizzas

9 pizza bruschettina (270g), split in half
⅓ cup (85g) bottled tomato sauce
1¼ cups (125g) coarsely grated mozzarella cheese
2 baby red-skinned potatoes (130g), sliced thinly
1 tablespoon olive oil
1 clove garlic, crushed
1 tablespoon coarsely chopped fresh rosemary
1 tablespoon olive oil, extra
8 ounces (250g) lamb fillets
¼ cup (30g) pitted black olives, halved
1½ ounces (50g) feta cheese, crumbled
1 tablespoon fresh small flat-leaf parsley leaves

1 Preheat oven to 475°C. Oil two oven or pizza trays.
2 Place bread on trays; spread with sauce; sprinkle with mozzarella. Top pizza with potato, overlapping slightly; brush with oil. Sprinkle with garlic and rosemary; season.
3 Bake pizzas about 12 minutes or until potato is tender and bases are browned and crisp.
4 Meanwhile, heat extra oil in medium frying pan; cook lamb until browned and cooked as desired. Cover lamb; stand 5 minutes, then slice thinly.
5 Serve pizzas topped with lamb, olives, feta and parsley.

prep + cook time 25 minutes **makes** 18
nutritional count per piece 5.7g total fat (2.1g saturated fat); 463 cal; 7.9g carbohydrate; 6.6g protein; 0.6g fiber

asparagus and goat cheese party pizzas

¼ cup (60ml) olive oil

1 clove garlic, chopped finely

2 teaspoons fresh thyme leaves

6½ ounces (200g) ricotta cheese

4 ounces (120g) goat cheese, crumbled

1 pound (525g) asparagus, trimmed, halved lengthways

¼ cup loosely packed fresh parsley sprigs

pizza dough

1½ cups (225g) bread flour or plain (all-purpose) flour

1 teaspoon (4g) dried yeast

1 teaspoon superfine sugar

1 teaspoon fine table salt

1 tablespoon olive oil

½ cup (125ml) warm water, approximately

1 Make pizza dough.

2 Preheat oven to 475°F. Oil two oven trays; place in heated oven.

3 Divide dough in half; roll each half on floured surface into 6-inch x 16-inch rectangle. Place on trays.

4 Combine oil, garlic and half the thyme in small bowl; brush about two-thirds of the oil mixture over pizza bases. Top with both cheeses and asparagus. Brush with remaining oil mixture; sprinkle with remaining thyme, season.

5 Bake pizzas about 15 minutes or until bases are browned and crisp. Cut each pizza into 12 pieces. Serve sprinkled with parsley.

pizza dough Combine flour, yeast, sugar and salt in medium bowl; make a well in the center. Stir in oil and enough of the water to mix to a soft dough. Knead dough on floured surface about 10 minutes or until smooth and elastic. Place dough in large oiled bowl, cover; stand in a warm place about 1 hour or until dough doubles in size. Turn dough onto floured surface; knead until smooth.

prep + cook time 45 minutes (+ standing)
makes 24
nutritional count per piece 4.9g total fat (1.6g saturated fat); 344 cal; 6.3g carbohydrate; 3g protein; 0.7g fiber

You need 3 bunches of asparagus for this recipe.

The meatballs are made from Italian pork sausages, but you can experiment with sausages with different flavor combinations from your butcher. If your meat options are limited, pure pork sausages also work well.

meatball party pizzas

2 rectangular pizza bases, 6½-inches x
   10½-inches
⅔ cup (170g) bottled tomato sauce
2 cups (200g) coarsely grated mozzarella cheese
6½ ounces (200g) italian pork sausages
6½ ounces (200g) ground beef
2 cloves garlic, crushed
pinch dried chili flakes
½ teaspoon dried oregano
5 ounces (155g) roasted red bell pepper, drained,
   sliced thinly
¼ cup (20g) roasted almond slivers
¼ cup loosely packed fresh flat-leaf parsley leaves

1 Preheat oven to 475°F. Oil two oven trays.
2 Place pizza bases on trays. Spread bases with sauce; sprinkle with mozzarella.
3 Squeeze sausage meat from casings into medium bowl. Add beef, garlic, chili and oregano; mix well, season. Roll rounded teaspoons of mixture into balls. Place meatballs on pizza bases, in rows. Sprinkle red bell pepper between meatballs; season.
4 Bake pizzas about 15 minutes or until meatballs are cooked through and bases are browned and crisp.
5 Cut pizzas into squares with one meatball on each piece. Sprinkle pizzas with nuts and parsley.

prep + cook time 35 minutes **makes** 48
nutritional count per piece 2.8g total fat
(1.3g saturated fat); 65 cal; 6.1g carbohydrate;
3.6g protein; 0.6g fiber

haloumi, spinach and tomato party pizzas

12½ ounces (400g) baby spinach leaves
⅓ cup (40g) pitted black olives
4 ounces (125g) cherry tomatoes, halved
2 tablespoons fresh oregano leaves
2 cloves garlic, crushed
2 tablespoons olive oil
2½ ounces (70g) haloumi cheese, grated coarsely
2½ ounces (70g) feta cheese, crumbled

pizza dough
1½ cups (225g) bread flour or plain (all-purpose) flour
1 teaspoon (4g) dried yeast
1 teaspoon superfine sugar
1 teaspoon fine table salt
1 tablespoon olive oil
½ cup (125ml) warm water, approximately

1 Make pizza dough.
2 Meanwhile, boil, steam or microwave spinach until wilted; drain. Rinse under cold water; drain. Squeeze out excess water; chop spinach coarsely.
3 Preheat oven to 475°F. Oil two oven trays; place in heated oven.
4 Divide dough in half; roll each half on floured surface into 6-inch x 16-inch rectangle. Place on trays.
5 Combine olives, tomato, oregano, garlic and oil in small bowl; season to taste.
6 Divide spinach between bases; sprinkle with half the cheeses. Top with olive mixture; sprinkle with remaining cheeses.
7 Bake pizzas about 15 minutes or until bases are browned and crisp. Cut each pizza into 8 slices.

pizza dough Combine flour, yeast, sugar and salt in medium bowl; make a well in the center. Stir in oil and enough of the water to mix to a soft dough. Knead dough on floured surface about 10 minutes or until smooth and elastic. Place dough in large oiled bowl, cover; stand in a warm place about 1 hour or until dough doubles in size. Turn dough onto floured surface; knead until smooth.

prep + cook time 40 minutes (+ standing)
makes 16
nutritional count per piece 5.5g total fat (1.7g saturated fat); 106 cal; 9.7g carbohydrate; 3.7g protein; 1.4g fiber

Caramelized onion, also called onion jam, is available in jars from large supermarkets and delicatessens. We used a mild blue castello cheese.

pancetta, fig and blue cheese pizzettas

½ cup (110g) caramelized onion
4½ ounces (150g) mild blue cheese, cut into
   24 pieces
6 slices pancetta (90g), chopped coarsely
3 medium fresh figs (180g), each cut into
   8 wedges
½ cup loosely packed watercress sprigs

pizza dough
1½ cups (225g) bread flour or plain (all-purpose)
   flour
1 teaspoon (4g) dried yeast
1 teaspoon superfine sugar
1 teaspoon fine table salt
1 tablespoon olive oil
½ cup (125ml) warm water, approximately

1 Make pizza dough.
2 Preheat oven to 475°F. Oil two oven trays; place in heated oven.
3 Roll dough into a 16-inch square; using 3¼-inch round cutter, cut out 24 rounds, re-rolling scraps. Place on trays.
4 Spread 1 teaspoon of caramelized onion over each base; top each with a piece of cheese, sprinkle with pancetta.
5 Bake pizzettas about 10 minutes or until bases are browned and crisp.
6 Serve pizzettas topped with fig and watercress.

pizza dough Combine flour, yeast, sugar and salt in medium bowl; make a well in the center. Stir in oil and enough of the water to mix to a soft dough. Knead dough on floured surface about 10 minutes or until smooth and elastic. Place dough in large oiled bowl, cover; stand in a warm place about 1 hour or until dough doubles in size. Turn dough onto floured surface; knead until smooth.

prep + cook time 45 minutes (+ standing)
makes 24
nutritional count per pizzetta 3.6g total fat (1.6g saturated fat); 74 cal; 7.1g carbohydrate; 3.1g protein; 0.6g fiber

Roll the dough as thinly as you can and don't worry about uneven shapes, it gives the pizzettas a rustic charm. We used an arrabbiata-style pasta sauce for this recipe; it is a tomato-based sauce that has been infused with chili, onion, garlic and sometimes pancetta. You can use any bottled tomato sauce you like.

puttanesca pizzettas

⅔ cup (170g) bottled arrabbiata sauce
4 cloves garlic, sliced thinly
1 cup (80g) pitted black olives, halved
32 white anchovy fillets (80g)
1 tablespoon rinsed, drained capers
6½ ounces (200g) taleggio cheese, sliced thinly

pizza dough
2½ cups (375g) bread flour or plain (all-purpose) flour
2 teaspoons (7g) dried yeast
2 teaspoons superfine sugar
2 teaspoons fine table salt
2 tablespoons olive oil
1 cup (250ml) warm water, approximately

1 Make pizza dough.
2 Preheat oven to 475°F. Oil oven trays; place in heated oven.
3 Divide dough into 16 portions; roll portions into 4-inch x 6-inch ovals. Place on trays.
4 Spread bases with sauce; top with garlic, olives, anchovies, capers and cheese. Season.
5 Bake pizzettas about 10 minutes or until bases are browned and crisp.

pizza dough Combine flour, yeast, sugar and salt in medium bowl; make a well in the center. Stir in oil and enough of the water to mix to a soft dough. Knead dough on floured surface about 10 minutes or until smooth and elastic. Place dough in large oiled bowl, cover; stand in a warm place about 1 hour or until dough doubles in size. Turn dough onto floured surface; knead until smooth.

prep + cook time 45 minutes (+ standing)
makes 16
nutritional count per pizzetta 6.7g total fat (2.8g saturated fat); 168 cal; 19.5g carbohydrate; 6.6g protein; 1.3g fiber

Taleggio is a soft, full flavored Italian cheese that goes well with the flavors of these pizzettas. If you like, use bocconcini for a milder flavor.

White anchovy fillets are available from most delis.

red wine, pear and gorgonzola party pizzas

2 cups (500ml) dry red wine

⅓ cup (75g) superfine sugar

2 star anise

2 cinnamon sticks

1 vanilla bean, split

2 medium pears (460g), peeled

⅔ cup (50g) finely grated parmesan cheese

1 cup (100g) coarsely grated mozzarella cheese

3 ounces (100g) gorgonzola cheese, crumbled

¼ small radicchio (35g), shredded finely

poppy seed pizza dough

1½ cups (225g) bread flour or plain (all-purpose)
   flour

1 teaspoon (4g) dried yeast

1 teaspoon superfine sugar

1 teaspoon fine table salt

½ teaspoon poppy seeds

1 tablespoon olive oil

½ cup (125ml) warm water, approximately

1 Make poppy seed pizza dough.

2 Meanwhile, stir wine, sugar, star anise, cinnamon and vanilla bean in small saucepan over heat, without boiling, until sugar dissolves. Bring to the boil. Reduce heat; add pears and enough water to cover pears. Simmer, covered, about 1 hour or until pears are tender. Remove pears; reserve 1 cup of the poaching liquid, discard remaining liquid. When pears are cool enough to handle, slice thinly lengthways.

3 Return reserved poaching liquid to pan; boil, uncovered, about 10 minutes or until the syrup thickens slightly.

4 Preheat oven to 475°F. Oil two oven trays; place in heated oven.

5 Divide dough in half; roll each half on floured surface into 4¾-inch x 16-inch rectangle. Place on trays.

6 Sprinkle pizza bases with combined cheeses. Bake pizzas about 12 minutes or until bases are browned and crisp.

7 Top pizzas with pear, in single layer; sprinkle over radicchio. Bake about 3 minutes or until radicchio is wilted. Serve pizzas drizzled with syrup.

poppy seed pizza dough Combine flour, yeast, sugar, salt and seeds in medium bowl; make a well in the center. Stir in oil and enough of the water to mix to a soft dough. Knead dough on floured surface about 10 minutes or until smooth and elastic. Place dough in large oiled bowl, cover; stand in a warm place about 1 hour or until dough doubles in size. Turn dough onto floured surface; knead until smooth.

prep + cook time 2 hours 10 minutes (+ standing)
serves 10
nutritional count per serving 9.2g total fat (4.8g saturated fat); 231 cal; 26.8g carbohydrate; 9g protein; 1.5g fiber

To get the shredded lime rind, peel the lime, removing the white pith, then slice it lengthways into thin segments. Taramasalata is a thick dip made from fish roe, breadcrumbs and olive oil. It is available from the refrigerated section of supermarkets.

taramasalata and salmon roe pizzettas

12-inch round pizza base (220g)
1 teaspoon olive oil
¼ cup (50g) taramasalata
1½ tablespoons salmon roe
2 teaspoons finely shredded lime rind
½ lime, segmented, sliced thinly
24 small sprigs fresh dill

prep + cook time 20 minutes **makes** 24
nutritional count per pizzetta 1.1g total fat
(0.2g saturated fat); 36 cal; 5.1g carbohydrate;
1.2g protein; 0.5g fiber

1 Preheat oven to 475°F. Oil two oven trays; place in heated oven.
2 Brush pizza base with oil; cut 24 2-inch rounds from base, place on trays. Bake rounds about 5 minutes or until browned and crisp.
3 Spread rounds with taramasalata; top with salmon roe, lime rind, lime segments and dill.

glam
pizzas

lamb and pomegranate pizza

2 teaspoons olive oil

1 teaspoon finely grated lemon rind

¼ teaspoon ground cumin

pinch dried chili flakes

6½ ounces (200g) lamb fillets

½ cup (130g) hummus

⅔ cup (190g) yogurt

2 12-inch round pizza bases (440g)

1 medium (320g) pomegranate

½ cup each loosely packed fresh mint and
    coriander (cilantro) leaves

1 lemon, cut into wedges

1 Combine oil, rind, cumin and chili in small bowl; add lamb, turn to coat. Cover; refrigerate 20 minutes.

2 Meanwhile, combine hummus and half the yogurt in small bowl; season to taste.

3 Preheat oven to 475°F. Oil two oven or pizza trays; place in heated oven.

4 Place pizza bases on trays, spread with hummus mixture; bake about 10 minutes or until bases are browned and crisp.

5 Meanwhile, cook lamb on heated oiled grill plate (or grill or barbecue) until cooked as desired. Cover lamb; stand 5 minutes then slice thinly. Cut the pomegranate in half crossways; remove seeds with a teaspoon.

6 Top pizzas with lamb and herbs; sprinkle with pomegranate seeds, drizzle with remaining yogurt. Serve immediately; accompany with lemon wedges.

prep + cook time 45 minutes (+ refrigeration)
serves 6
nutritional count per serving 14.2g total fat (4.7g saturated fat); 412 cal; 48.8g carbohydrate; 18.1g protein; 7.2g fiber

gorgonzola, ham and sticky balsamic pizza

⅔ cup (170g) bottled tomato sauce

¼ cup (20g) finely grated parmesan cheese

½ cup (50g) finely grated mozzarella cheese

2 ounces (60g) gorgonzola cheese, crumbled

1½ ounces (50g) thinly sliced ham

¼ cup (60ml) balsamic vinegar

¼ cup (60ml) water

1½ tablespoons lemon juice

1 tablespoon light brown sugar

1 ounce (30g) arugula

pizza dough

1½ cups (225g) bread flour or plain (all-purpose) flour

1 teaspoon (4g) dried yeast

1 teaspoon superfine sugar

1 teaspoon fine table salt

1 tablespoon olive oil

½ cup (125ml) warm water, approximately

1 Make pizza dough.

2 Preheat oven to 475°F. Oil two oven trays; place in heated oven.

3 Divide dough in half; roll each half on floured surface into 10-inch round. Place on trays.

4 Spread pizza bases with sauce; top with cheeses and ham.

5 Bake pizzas about 15 minutes or until bases are browned and crisp.

6 Meanwhile, combine vinegar, the water, juice and sugar in small saucepan; stir over heat, without boiling, until sugar dissolves. Bring to the boil. Reduce heat; simmer, uncovered, about 10 minutes or until syrup thickens slightly.

7 Serve pizzas topped with arugula and drizzled with syrup.

pizza dough Combine flour, yeast, sugar and salt in medium bowl; make a well in the center. Stir in oil and enough of the water to mix to a soft dough. Knead dough on floured surface about 10 minutes or until smooth and elastic. Place dough in large oiled bowl, cover; stand in a warm place about 1 hour or until dough doubles in size. Turn dough onto floured surface; knead until smooth.

prep + cook time 50 minutes (+ standing) **serves** 4
nutritional count per serving 16.9g total fat (7.4g saturated fat); 396 cal; 41.6g carbohydrate; 17.4g protein; 2.8g fiber

Use store-bought balsamic glaze, if you like.

roasted beets, onion and rosemary pizza

1 large fresh beet (200g), trimmed, peeled,
  chopped coarsely
2 tablespoons olive oil
1 medium red onion (170g), cut into wedges
2 tablespoons balsamic vinegar
1 tablespoon light brown sugar
⅔ cup (170g) bottled tomato sauce
1 cup (100g) pizza cheese
4 ounces (125g) feta cheese, crumbled
2 tablespoons pine nuts
2 teaspoons finely chopped fresh rosemary
1 cup finely shredded radicchio

pizza dough

1½ cups (225g) bread flour or plain (all-purpose)
  flour
1 teaspoon (4g) dried yeast
1 teaspoon superfine sugar
1 teaspoon fine table salt
1 tablespoon olive oil
½ cup (125ml) warm water, approximately

1 Make pizza dough.
2 Meanwhile, preheat oven to 350°F.
3 Combine beet and 2 teaspoons of the oil in small shallow baking dish, season; roast, uncovered, about 30 minutes or until tender. Remove from oven.
4 Increase oven temperature to 475°F. Oil two oven or pizza trays; place in heated oven.

5 Meanwhile, heat 2 teaspoons of the oil in medium frying pan; cook onion, stirring, until softened. Add vinegar and sugar; cook, stirring, about 5 minutes or until liquid has evaporated and onion is caramelized. Remove from heat.
6 Divide dough in half; roll each half on floured surface into a 12-inch round. Place on trays.
7 Spread bases with sauce; top with cheeses, beet, onion and nuts.
8 Bake pizzas about 15 minutes or until bases are browned and crisp.
9 Meanwhile, combine remaining oil and rosemary in small saucepan; warm over low heat, about 2 minutes or until fragrant. Remove from heat; cool 5 minutes.
10 Serve pizzas drizzled with rosemary oil; sprinkle with radicchio.

pizza dough Combine flour, yeast, sugar and salt in medium bowl; make a well in the center. Stir in oil and enough of the water to mix to a soft dough. Knead dough on floured surface about 10 minutes or until smooth and elastic. Place dough in large oiled bowl, cover; stand in a warm place about 1 hour or until dough doubles in size. Turn dough onto floured surface; knead until smooth.

prep + cook time 35 minutes (+ standing) **serves** 4
nutritional count per serving 32.9g total fat
(10.7g saturated fat); 581 cal; 47.7g carbohydrate;
21.4g protein; 5.6g fiber

salami, mozzarella and oregano pizza

⅔ cup (170g) bottled tomato sauce

3 ounces (100g) buffalo mozzarella cheese, chopped coarsely

2 ounces (60g) thinly sliced hot sopressa salami, chopped coarsely

2 tablespoons olive oil

2 cloves garlic, sliced thinly

2 tablespoons fresh oregano leaves

pizza dough

1½ cups (225g) bread flour or plain (all-purpose) flour

1 teaspoon (4g) dried yeast

1 teaspoon superfine sugar

1 teaspoon fine table salt

1 tablespoon olive oil

½ cup (125ml) warm water, approximately

1 Make pizza dough.

2 Preheat oven to 475°F. Oil two oven trays; place in heated oven.

3 Divide dough in half; roll each half on floured surface into 8-inch x 12-inch ovals. Place on trays.

4 Spread bases with sauce; top with cheese and the salami.

5 Bake pizzas about 15 minutes or until bases are browned and crisp.

6 Meanwhile, combine oil, garlic and oregano in small saucepan; cook, over low heat, until oregano is crisp and garlic is browned lightly. Remove from heat; cool 5 minutes.

7 Serve pizzas drizzled with garlic and oregano oil.

pizza dough Combine flour, yeast, sugar and salt in medium bowl; make a well in the center. Stir in oil and enough of the water to mix to a soft dough. Knead dough on floured surface about 10 minutes or until smooth and elastic. Place dough in large oiled bowl, cover; stand in a warm place about 1 hour or until dough doubles in size. Turn dough onto floured surface; knead until smooth.

prep + cook time 40 minutes (+ standing) **serves** 4
nutritional count per serving 24.4g total fat (6.4g saturated fat); 433 cal; 38.4g carbohydrate; 13.8g protein; 3.1g fiber

Sumac is a deep-red or purple spice ground from berries, and is used in Middle-Eastern dishes to add a lemony taste to salads or meat.

lamb with quinoa pizzettas

1 teaspoon sumac

1 clove garlic, crushed

1 tablespoon olive oil

3 lamb fillets (300g)

1 tablespoon quinoa, rinsed, drained

⅓ cup (80ml) water

½ cup (140g) greek-style yogurt

1 tablespoon lemon juice

¼ cup coarsely chopped fresh flat-leaf parsley

½ cup (70g) roasted unsalted pistachios, chopped finely

½ cup (60g) pitted green olives, chopped finely

1 fresh long green chili, chopped finely

2 teaspoons finely grated lemon rind

2 tablespoons olive oil, extra

4 pita pocket breads (300g)

¾ cup (60g) coarsely grated pecorino cheese

1 Combine sumac, garlic and oil in medium bowl; add lamb, turn to coat. Cover; refrigerate 30 minutes.

2 Meanwhile, combine quinoa and the water in small saucepan; bring to the boil. Reduce heat; simmer, covered, about 12 minutes or until water is absorbed and quinoa is tender.

3 Combine yogurt, juice and 1 tablespoon of the parsley in small bowl.

4 Combine quinoa, nuts, olives, chili, rind, extra oil and remaining parsley in small bowl; season to taste.

5 Preheat oven to 425°F.

6 Place bread on oiled wire rack over oven tray; sprinkle with cheese. Bake about 10 minutes or until breads are browned and crisp.

7 Meanwhile, cook lamb on heated oiled grill plate (or grill or barbecue) until cooked as desired. Cover lamb; stand 5 minutes then slice thinly.

8 Serve breads topped with quinoa, lamb and yogurt mixture.

prep + cook time 55 minutes (+ refrigeration)
makes 4
nutritional count per pizzetta 33.9g total fat (9.2g saturated fat); 565 cal; 32.7g carbohydrate; 30.5g protein; 3.5g fiber

slow-roasted moroccan lamb pizza

1 tablespoon olive oil

3 french-trimmed lamb shanks (600g)

1 small brown onion (100g), chopped finely

½ teaspoon ground cumin

pinch saffron threads

1 teaspoon ras el hanout

1 teaspoon each ground ginger and cinnamon

½ teaspoon ground white pepper

12½ ounces (400g) canned chopped tomatoes

1½ cups (375ml) vegetable stock

2 tablespoons dried currants

¾ cup (75g) pizza cheese

2 tablespoons slivered almonds, roasted

6 ounces (185g) persian feta cheese, drained

¼ cup (50g) preserved lemon rind, chopped finely

¼ cup loosely packed fresh cilantro

saffron pizza dough

1½ cups (225g) bread flour or plain (all-purpose) flour

1 teaspoon (4g) dried yeast

1 teaspoon superfine sugar

1 teaspoon fine table salt

pinch saffron threads

1 tablespoon olive oil

½ cup (125ml) warm water, approximately

1 Preheat oven to 300°F.

2 Heat oil in medium flameproof dish; cook lamb until browned, remove from dish. Add onion to dish; cook, stirring, until softened. Add spices; cook, stirring, until fragrant. Return lamb to dish with undrained tomatoes, stock and currants; bring to the boil. Cover dish, transfer to oven; cook about 3 hours or until lamb is almost falling off the bone. Remove from oven.

3 Meanwhile, make saffron pizza dough.

4 Increase oven temperature to 475°F. Oil two oven or pizza trays; place in heated oven.

5 Remove lamb from dish; skim fat from the surface of juices in dish. To make sauce, return dish with juices to stove top; bring to the boil. Reduce heat; simmer, uncovered, about 10 minutes or until sauce is thickened. Season to taste.

6 Meanwhile, remove meat from bones; shred meat coarsely, cover to keep warm.

7 Divide dough in half; roll each half on floured surface into a 12-inch round. Place on trays.

8 Spread bases with 1 cup of the sauce; sprinkle with pizza cheese and lamb. Bake about 15 minutes or until bases are browned and crisp.

9 Serve pizzas topped with nuts, feta, rind and coriander leaves.

saffron pizza dough Combine flour, yeast, sugar, salt and saffron in medium bowl; make a well in the center. Stir in oil and enough of the water to mix to a soft dough. Knead dough on floured surface about 10 minutes or until smooth and elastic. Place dough in large oiled bowl, cover; stand in a warm place about 1 hour or until dough doubles in size. Turn dough onto floured surface; knead until smooth.

prep + cook time 3 hours 30 minutes (+ standing)
serves 4
nutritional count per serving 26.4g total fat (7.8g saturated fat); 554 cal; 45.9g carbohydrate; 30.8g protein; 4.7g fiber

Use any soft feta cheese instead of persian feta, if you like. Don't overload the pizzas with lamb as they will become soggy. Any leftover lamb and sauce can be frozen in an airtight container for up to three months.

Caramelized onion, also called onion jam, is available in jars from large supermarkets and most delicatessens.

potato and caramelized onion pizza

½ cup (110g) caramelized onion
⅔ cup (70g) coarsely grated mozzarella cheese
2 small potatoes (240g), unpeeled
½ cup (40g) finely grated parmesan cheese
2 tablespoons olive oil
2 teaspoons fresh thyme leaves
2 cloves garlic, crushed

pizza dough
1½ cups (225g) bread flour or plain (all-purpose)
   flour
1 teaspoon (4g) dried yeast
1 teaspoon superfine sugar
1 teaspoon fine table salt
1 tablespoon olive oil
½ cup (125ml) warm water, approximately

1 Make pizza dough.
2 Preheat oven to 475°F. Oil two oven or pizza trays; place in heated oven.
3 Divide dough in half; roll each half on floured surface into 6-inch x 14-inch slipper shapes. Place on trays.
4 Spread bases with caramelized onion; sprinkle with mozzarella. Using a mandoline or V-slicer, cut potato into paper thin slices. Place potato, slightly overlapping, onto pizzas; sprinkle with parmesan. Combine oil, thyme and garlic in small bowl; drizzle over pizzas.
5 Bake pizzas about 15 minutes or until base is browned and crisp.

pizza dough Combine flour, yeast, sugar and salt in medium bowl; make a well in the center. Stir in oil and enough of the water to mix to a soft dough. Knead dough on floured surface about 10 minutes or until smooth and elastic. Place dough in large oiled bowl, cover; stand in a warm place about 1 hour or until dough doubles in size. Turn dough onto floured surface; knead until smooth.

prep + cook time 45 minutes (+ standing) **serves** 6
nutritional count per serving 12.8g total fat (3.2g saturated fat); 270 cal; 29.6g carbohydrate; 7.8g protein; 2.2g fiber

For a more authentic Italian flavor, use the same amount of taleggio cheese instead of the brie.

wild mushroom, brie and walnut pizza

2 tablespoons olive oil
9½ ounces (300g) oyster mushrooms, trimmed
9½ ounces (300g) shimeji mushrooms, trimmed
6½ ounces (200g) fresh shiitake mushrooms,
  quartered
2 cloves garlic, crushed
1 cup loosely packed fresh flat-leaf parsley leaves
½ cup (130g) bottled tomato sauce
⅔ cup (70g) coarsely grated mozzarella cheese
½ cup (50g) walnuts, roasted, chopped coarsely
6½ ounces (200g) brie cheese, cut into 12 wedges

pizza dough
1½ cups (225g) bread flour or plain (all-purpose)
  flour
1 teaspoon (4g) dried yeast
1 teaspoon superfine sugar
1 teaspoon fine table salt
1 tablespoon olive oil
½ cup (125ml) warm water, approximately

1 Make pizza dough.
2 Preheat oven to 475°F. Oil two oven or pizza trays; place in heated oven.
3 Heat oil in large frying pan; cook mushrooms and garlic, stirring occasionally, about 3 minutes or until mushrooms are tender. Add parsley; cook, stirring, 1 minute. Remove from heat; season to taste.
4 Divide dough in half; roll each half on floured surface into a 12-inch round. Place on trays.
5 Spread bases with sauce; sprinkle with mozzarella. Top with mushrooms, nuts and brie.
6 Bake pizzas about 15 minutes or until bases are browned and crisp.

pizza dough Combine flour, yeast, sugar and salt in medium bowl; make a well in the center. Stir in oil and enough of the water to mix to a soft dough. Knead dough on floured surface about 10 minutes or until smooth and elastic. Place dough in large oiled bowl, cover; stand in a warm place about 1 hour or until dough doubles in size. Turn dough onto floured surface; knead until smooth.

prep + cook time 45 minutes (+ standing) **serves** 6
nutritional count per serving 28g total fat
(9.5g saturated fat); 448 cal; 26.5g carbohydrate;
18.9g protein; 8.9g fiber

Reserve some of the fronds from the fennel before slicing and sprinkle over the pizzas to serve. You can use sour cream instead of crème fraîche.

smoked salmon and crème fraîche pizza

1½ cups (360g) ricotta cheese
2 tablespoons olive oil
1½ tablespoons black fish roe
2 tablespoons finely chopped fresh chives
9½ ounces (300g) thinly sliced smoked salmon
1 baby fennel (130g), sliced finely
1 cup loosely packed watercress sprigs
½ cup (120g) crème fraîche
1 lemon, cut into wedges

pizza dough
1½ cups (225g) bread flour or plain (all-purpose)
    flour
1 teaspoon (4g) dried yeast
1 teaspoon superfine sugar
1 teaspoon fine table salt
1 tablespoon olive oil
½ cup (125ml) warm water, approximately

1 Place cheese in muslin or paper towel-lined sieve over medium bowl. Drain for at least 1 hour. After draining you should have 1 cup of cheese.
2 Meanwhile, make pizza dough.
3 Preheat oven to 475°F. Oil two oven or pizza trays; place in heated oven.

4 Divide dough in half; roll each half on floured surface into a 12-inch round. Place on trays.
5 Spread bases with cheese. Bake about 10 minutes or until bases are browned and crisp.
6 Meanwhile, combine oil, roe and chives in a small bowl.
7 Serve pizzas topped with salmon, fennel, watercress and crème fraîche; drizzle with the oil and roe mixture, serve with lemon wedges.

pizza dough Combine flour, yeast, sugar and salt in medium bowl; make a well in the center. Stir in oil and enough of the water to mix to a soft dough. Knead dough on floured surface about 10 minutes or until smooth and elastic. Place dough in large oiled bowl, cover; stand in a warm place about 1 hour or until dough doubles in size. Turn dough onto floured surface; knead until smooth.

prep + cook time 45 minutes (+ standing) **serves** 6
nutritional count per serving 26.8g total fat (11.4g saturated fat); 436 cal; 25.3g carbohydrate; 22.8g protein; 2.1g fiber

shrimp, squid and salsa verde pizza

12 uncooked medium shrimp (540g)

2 small cleaned squid (150g), sliced thinly into rings

2 tablespoons olive oil

2 teaspoons finely grated lemon rind

½ teaspoon dried chili flakes

2 cloves garlic, crushed

1 cup (260g) bottled tomato sauce

1 cup (100g) coarsely grated mozzarella cheese

1 drained roasted red bell pepper (60g), sliced thickly

pizza dough

1½ cups (225g) bread flour or plain (all-purpose) flour

1 teaspoon (4g) dried yeast

1 teaspoon superfine sugar

1 teaspoon fine table salt

1 tablespoon olive oil

½ cup (125ml) warm water, approximately

salsa verde

½ cup loosely packed fresh flat-leaf parsley leaves

¼ cup loosely packed fresh mint leaves

¼ cup (60ml) olive oil

2 teaspoons rinsed, drained baby capers

2 teaspoons lemon juice

1 clove garlic, quartered

1 Make pizza dough.

2 Meanwhile, shell and devein shrimp; halve shrimp lengthways. Combine shrimp, squid, oil, rind, chili and garlic in medium bowl; season.

3 Preheat oven to 475°F. Oil two oven or pizza trays; place in heated oven.

4 Divide dough in half; roll each half on floured surface into 8-inch x 10-inch rectangle. Place on trays.

5 Spread bases with sauce; top with cheese, red bell pepper and seafood mixture.

6 Bake about 15 minutes or until bases are browned and crisp.

7 Meanwhile, make salsa verde. Serve pizzas drizzled with salsa.

pizza dough Combine flour, yeast, sugar and salt in medium bowl; make a well in the center. Stir in oil and enough of the water to mix to a soft dough. Knead dough on floured surface about 10 minutes or until smooth and elastic. Place dough in large oiled bowl, cover; stand in a warm place about 1 hour or until dough doubles in size. Turn dough onto floured surface; knead until smooth.

salsa verde Blend or process ingredients until smooth; season to taste.

prep + cook time 40 minutes (+ standing) **serves** 6
nutritional count per serving 23.9g total fat (5.3g saturated fat); 420 cal; 27.4g carbohydrate; 22.5g protein; 3g fiber

To save time, buy shelled and deveined shrimp and calamari rings from your local fish supplier. Some major supermarkets also have a fresh seafood section.

kids' pizzas

salami and pineapple pizzas

2 12-inch round pizza bases (440g)

1 cup (260g) bottled tomato sauce

1½ cups (150g) coarsely grated mozzarella cheese

14½ ounces (440g) canned pineapple rings in natural juice, drained

5 ounces (155g) salami, sliced thinly

1 Preheat oven to 425°F. Oil two oven or pizza trays; place in heated oven.

2 Place pizza bases on trays; spread with sauce, top with cheese, pineapple and salami.

3 Bake pizzas about 15 minutes or until bases are browned and crisp.

prep + cook time 30 minutes serves 4
nutritional count per serving 15.4g total fat (6.5g saturated fat); 403 cal; 46.1g carbohydrate; 17.9g protein; 4.3g fiber

Break the cheesy crusts off the pizza and dip into the runny egg yolk. String cheese is a shelf-stable processed cheese found alongside children's snack foods in supermarkets. String cheese keeps its shape when cooked.

bacon and egg cheesy crust pizzas

1 teaspoon olive oil
2 rindless bacon slices (130g), chopped coarsely
10 ¾-ounce string cheeses, halved lengthways
⅓ cup (85g) bottled tomato sauce
2 tablespoons smoky barbecue sauce
⅔ cup (70g) pizza cheese
2 eggs

pizza dough
1½ cups (225g) bread flour or plain (all-purpose) flour
1 teaspoon (4g) dried yeast
1 teaspoon superfine sugar
1 teaspoon fine table salt
1 tablespoon olive oil
½ cup (125ml) warm water, approximately

1 Make pizza dough.
2 Heat oil in large frying pan; cook bacon, stirring, until browned lightly. Drain on paper towels.
3 Preheat oven to 475°F. Oil two oven or pizza trays; place in heated oven.
4 Divide dough in half; roll each half on floured surface into a 12-inch round. Place on trays. Place string cheeses, end-to-end, along the edge of each round, leaving a ¾ inch border. Lift edge of dough over string cheeses to enclose, press firmly to seal.
5 Combine sauces in small bowl; spread pizza bases with sauce, season. Top with bacon; sprinkle with pizza cheese.
6 Bake pizzas 10 minutes; remove from oven. Carefully crack eggs onto pizzas. Bake pizzas about 5 minutes or until egg is cooked.

pizza dough Combine flour, yeast, sugar and salt in medium bowl; make a well in the center. Stir in oil and enough of the water to mix to a soft dough. Knead dough on floured surface about 10 minutes or until smooth and elastic. Place dough in large oiled bowl, cover; stand in a warm place about 1 hour or until dough doubles in size. Turn dough onto floured surface; knead until smooth.

prep + cook time 50 minutes (+ standing) **serves** 4
nutritional count per serving 29.5g total fat (13.8g saturated fat); 560 cal; 41.9g carbohydrate; 31.1g protein; 2.4g fiber

This is great party food for older kids; marinade the meat and make the avocado salsa ahead of time. Get the kids to top their own pizzas.

tex-mex pizzas

1 tablespoon olive oil
1 teaspoon ground cumin
1 teaspoon smoked paprika
4 lamb fillets (400g)
1 trimmed corn from one cob (250g)
1 small avocado (200g), chopped coarsely
4 ounces (125g) cherry tomatoes, quartered
1 green onion (scallion), sliced thinly
¼ cup each coarsely chopped fresh mint and
   cilantro
1 tablespoon lime juice
4 large flour tortillas (450g)
1¼ cups (150g) coarsely grated cheddar cheese
¾ cup (180g) light sour cream

1 Combine oil and spices in medium bowl; add lamb, turn to coat. Cover; refrigerate until ready to cook.
2 Cook corn on heated oiled grill plate (or grill or barbecue), until browned lightly and tender. Remove from heat; when cool enough to handle remove kernels from cob.
3 Cook lamb on heated oiled grill plate until browned and cooked as desired. Cover lamb; stand 5 minutes then slice thinly.
4 Meanwhile, to make avocado salsa, combine corn, avocado, tomato, onion, herbs and juice in medium bowl; season to taste.
5 Cut 24 3¾-inch rounds from tortillas.
6 Cook tortilla rounds on heated grill plate 1 minute; turn tortillas, sprinkle with cheese. Cook 1 minute or until cheese melts.
7 Serve pizzas topped with lamb, avocado salsa and sour cream.

prep + cook time 35 minutes **makes** 24
nutritional count per pizza 6.8g total fat
(3.1g saturated fat); 107 cal; 4.7g carbohydrate;
6.5g protein; 0.8g fiber

Get the kids to cut out the pineapple shapes – metal cookie cutters are best for this. Or, cut the pizza base any shape you like – funny face, star, lady beetle, moon – and use the pineapple for facial features (eyes, nose and mouth), lady-beetle spots or a man on the moon.

ham and pineapple pizza pictures

2 12-inch round pizza bases (440g)
1 small pineapple (900g), sliced thinly
⅓ cup (90g) pizza sauce
1½ cups (150g) pizza cheese
5 ounces (155g) thinly sliced ham,
   chopped coarsely

1 Preheat oven to 475°F. Oil two oven or pizza trays; place in heated oven.
2 Use cookie cutters to cut shapes from pineapple.
3 Place pizza bases on trays. Spread bases with sauce; top with cheese and ham, then pineapple shapes.
4 Bake pizzas about 12 minutes or until bases are browned and crisp.

prep + cook time 35 minutes **serves** 4
nutritional count per serving 16.2g total fat (6.6g saturated fat); 673 cal; 100.5g carbohydrate; 35g protein; 9.6g fiber

With few ingredients and minimal preparation required, this is the ideal dish for a light Sunday dinner in front of the television.

chicken and mango tortillas

8 8-inch flour tortillas (400g)
2 tablespoons olive oil
2 cups (320g) shredded barbecued chicken
2 cups (240g) coarsely grated cheddar cheese

mango salsa
1 large mango (600g), chopped finely
1 green onion (scallion), chopped finely
⅓ cup coarsely chopped fresh cilantro

1 Preheat oven to 400°F. Oil two oven or pizza trays; place in heated oven.
2 Place one tortilla on board; brush with a little oil. Turn tortilla over; sprinkle ¼ cup of the chicken and ¼ cup of the cheese over one half of tortilla, season. Fold tortilla in half to enclose filling, press edges firmly. Repeat to make a total of 8 tortillas. Place on trays.
3 Bake tortillas about 12 minutes or until browned lightly and crisp.
4 Meanwhile, make mango salsa.
5 Cut each tortilla into 4 wedges; serve with salsa.

mango salsa Combine ingredients in small bowl.

prep + cook time 45 minutes **serves** 4
nutritional count per serving 41.5g total fat (17.1g saturated fat); 750 cal; 48.2g carbohydrate; 44.2g protein; 4.6g fiber

chicken and roasted squash pizzas

½ butternut squash (750g), chopped coarsely

1 tablespoon olive oil

2 cups (320g) shredded barbecued chicken

½ teaspoon cajun seasoning

2 12-inch round pizza bases (440g)

1 cup (260g) bottled tomato sauce

1½ cups (150g) coarsely grated mozzarella cheese

¼ cup coarsely chopped fresh flat-leaf parsley

1 Preheat oven to 400°F.

2 Combine squash and oil in small baking dish, season; roast, uncovered, about 15 minutes or until squash is tender. Cool.

3 Increase oven temperature to 425°F. Oil two oven or pizza trays; place in heated oven.

4 Combine chicken and seasoning in medium bowl.

5 Place pizza bases on tray, spread with sauce; top with cheese, squash and chicken.

6 Bake pizzas about 15 minutes or until bases are browned and crisp and chicken is heated through. Serve sprinkled with parsley.

prep + cook time 30 minutes **serves** 4
nutritional count per serving 25.8g total fat (9g saturated fat); 726 cal; 73.1g carbohydrate; 46g protein; 8.4g fiber

sausage and mushroom pizzas

8 4½-inch round pizza bases (440g)

½ cup (140g) barbecue sauce

1½ cups (150g) coarsely grated mozzarella cheese

4 ounces (125g) button mushrooms, sliced thinly

½ medium red bell pepper (100g), sliced thinly

2 thick italian pork sausages (240g)

1 Preheat oven to 425°F. Oil two oven or pizza trays; place in heated oven.

2 Place pizza bases on trays, spread with sauce; top with cheese, mushrooms and red bell pepper, season. Squeeze sausage meat from casings; drop small pieces of meat on top of pizzas.

3 Bake pizzas about 15 minutes or until bases are browned and crisp.

prep + cook time 30 minutes makes 8
nutritional count per pizza 13g total fat (5.6g saturated fat); 334 cal; 38.6g carbohydrate; 14.3g protein; 3.2g fiber

We used 6-inch squares of baking paper to line the muffin pan. These scrolls are great for school lunchboxes and after-school snacks. Wrap scrolls individually in plastic and freeze for up to one month.

ham, cheese and zucchini pizza scrolls

½ cup (130g) sundried tomato pesto
5 ounces (155g) thinly sliced ham, chopped
 coarsely
1 cup (120g) coarsely grated cheddar cheese

zucchini dough
3 teaspoons (10g) dried yeast
1 teaspoon fine table salt
2 teaspoons superfine sugar
3⅓ cups (485g) plain (all-purpose) flour
1 large zucchini (150g), grated coarsely
¼ cup (20g) finely grated parmesan cheese
1 tablespoon olive oil
¾ cup (180ml) warm water, approximately

1 Make zucchini dough.
2 Preheat oven to 425°F. Line 2 x 6-hole (¾-cup/ 180ml) texas muffin pans with paper baking cups.
3 Roll dough on floured surface into 12-inch x 20-inch rectangle. Spread dough with pesto; sprinkle with ham and cheese.

4 Starting at one long side, roll dough tightly. Trim edges. Cut roll into 12 slices; place slices, cut-side up, into pan holes. Stand in warm place about 40 minutes or until doubled in size.
5 Bake scrolls about 20 minutes or until browned lightly. Stand scrolls in pans 5 minutes; turn, top-side up, onto wire rack to cool.

zucchini dough Combine yeast, salt, sugar, flour, zucchini and cheese in large bowl; make a well in the center. Stir in oil and enough of the water to mix to a soft dough. Knead dough on floured surface about 10 minutes or until smooth and elastic. Place dough in large oiled bowl, cover; stand in a warm place about 1 hour or until dough doubles in size. Turn dough onto floured surface; knead until smooth.

prep + cook time 1 hour (+ standing) **makes** 12
nutritional count per scroll 10.8g total fat (3.9g saturated fat); 268 cal; 30.2g carbohydrate; 11.5g protein; 2g fiber

apple, pecan and maple dessert pizza

2 small apples (260g), peeled, cored, sliced thinly
¾ cup (30g) pecans, chopped coarsely
2 tablespoons light brown sugar
¼ teaspoon ground cinnamon
¾ ounce (20g) butter, chopped finely
¼ cup (60ml) pure maple syrup

pizza dough
1½ cups (225g) bread flour or plain (all-purpose) flour
1 teaspoon (4g) dried yeast
1 teaspoon superfine sugar
1 teaspoon fine table salt
1 tablespoon olive oil
½ cup (125ml) warm water, approximately

almond filling
1 ounce (30g) butter
¼ teaspoon vanilla extract
¼ cup (55g) superfine sugar
1 egg
1 tablespoon plain (all-purpose) flour
⅔ cup (80g) ground almonds

1 Make pizza dough. Make almond filling.
2 Preheat oven to 475°F. Grease two oven or pizza trays; place in heated oven.
3 Divide dough in half; roll each half on floured surface into a 12-inch round. Place on trays. Top each pizza base with a sheet of baking paper and another oven tray.
4 Bake bases 7 minutes; remove from oven, remove top tray and baking paper. Spread bases with filling; top with apple and nuts, sprinkle with sugar and cinnamon, dot with butter. Bake about 15 minutes or until bases are browned and crisp.
5 Drizzle pizzas with syrup; serve with ice-cream.

pizza dough Combine flour, yeast, sugar and salt in medium bowl; make a well in the center. Stir in oil and enough of the water to mix to a soft dough. Knead dough on floured surface about 10 minutes or until smooth and elastic. Place dough in large oiled bowl, cover; stand in a warm place about 1 hour or until dough doubles in size. Turn dough onto floured surface; knead until smooth.

almond filling Beat butter, extract and sugar in small bowl with electric mixer until light and fluffy. Add egg; beat until combined. Stir in flour and ground almonds.

prep + cook time 50 minutes (+ standing) **serves** 4
nutritional count per serving 33.3g total fat (9g saturated fat); 652 cal; 75.8g carbohydrate; 12.3g protein; 4.9g fiber

You need four oven or pizza trays for this recipe, or you could make just one pizza at a time.
Stop the apple from browning by putting the slices into a bowl of cold water combined with the juice of half a lemon; drain the slices well before arranging them on the pizzas.

This recipe is gluten-free; however, if you decide to use pre-made packaged caramel popcorn, check the label carefully.

gluten-free strawberry bliss bomb pizzas

1 teaspoon vegetable oil
1 tablespoon popping corn
¼ cup (30g) pecans, chopped finely
1½ ounces (50g) butter
1 tablespoon honey
⅓ cup (75g) superfine sugar
8 ounces (250g) ricotta cheese
2 tablespoons cream cheese, softened
1 tablespoon finely grated orange rind
1 tablespoon confectioners' sugar
2 8¾-inch round gluten-free pizza bases (345g)
8 ounces (250g) strawberries, halved
2 tablespoons small fresh mint leaves

1 Heat oil in small saucepan; add popping corn, cover. Reduce heat; cook corn, covered, over medium heat, until corn starts popping. Reduce heat; cook, covered, over low heat, shaking pan occasionally, until popping stops. Sprinkle popcorn, in single layer, on heatproof tray; sprinkle nuts over popcorn.
2 Stir butter, honey and superfine sugar in small saucepan over low heat until sugar dissolves. Bring to the boil. Reduce heat; simmer, uncovered, about 5 minutes or until mixture is caramel in color.

3 Working quickly, pour the caramel mixture evenly over popcorn; use two lightly oiled metal spoons to turn popcorn to coat evenly with the caramel. When popcorn is cool enough to handle, use hands to separate popcorn pieces.
4 Preheat oven to 475°F. Grease two oven or pizza trays; place in heated oven.
5 Combine cheeses, rind and confectioners' sugar in medium bowl. Place pizza bases on trays; spread bases with cheese mixture.
6 Bake pizzas 10 minutes. Top pizzas with strawberries; bake about 5 minutes or until bases are browned and crisp.
7 Top pizzas with caramel popcorn and mint; dust with a little extra sifted confectioners' sugar before serving.

prep + cook time 1 hour **serves** 4
nutritional count per serving 23.6g total fat (9.8g saturated fat); 507 cal; 78.6g carbohydrate; 11.2g protein; 6.5g fiber

pizza express

greek pizza

2 12-inch round pizza bases (440g)
¾ cup (195g) bottled tomato sauce
1 medium red bell pepper (200g), sliced thinly
5 ounces (155g) feta cheese, crumbled
½ cup (40g) pitted black olives
1 teaspoon dried oregano
1 tablespoon olive oil

1 Preheat oven to 475°F. Oil two oven or pizza trays; place in heated oven for 5 minutes.
2 Place pizza bases on trays, spread with sauce; top with red bell pepper, cheese and olives. Sprinkle with oregano; drizzle with oil, season.
3 Bake pizzas about 15 minutes or until bases are browned and crisp.

prep + cook time 30 minutes **serves** 4
nutritional count per serving 18.7g total fat (7.2g saturated fat); 517 cal; 66g carbohydrate; 18.3g protein; 5.7g fiber

mexican pizza

1 tablespoon olive oil

12½ ounces (400g) ground beef

1 ounce (30g) taco seasoning

¾ cup (195g) bottled tomato sauce

2 12-inch round pizza bases (440g)

1 small green bell pepper (150g), sliced thinly

¼ cup (60g) coarsely chopped pickled jalapeño
   chilies

1 cup (100g) pizza cheese

salsa

1 small green bell pepper (150g), chopped finely

1 large tomato (220g), chopped finely

1 small red onion (100g), chopped finely

¼ cup finely chopped fresh cilantro

1 Preheat oven to 475°F. Oil two oven or pizza trays; place in heated oven.

2 Heat oil in large frying pan; cook beef, stirring, about 3 minutes or until browned. Stir in seasoning; cook, stirring, about 1 minute or until fragrant. Stir in sauce; remove from heat, season.

3 Place pizza bases on trays; spread with beef mixture. Top with green bell pepper and chili; sprinkle with cheese.

4 Bake pizzas about 15 minutes or until bases are browned and crisp.

5 Meanwhile, make salsa. Serve pizzas sprinkled with salsa.

salsa Combine ingredients in small bowl.

prep + cook time 35 minutes **serves** 4
nutritional count per serving 22.7g total fat
(8.5g saturated fat); 646 cal; 66g carbohydrate;
40g protein; 8.6g fiber

Australian pizzas are characterized by the inclusion of bacon and egg, making them a perfect treat for brunch.

australian pizza

2 12-inch round pizza bases (440g)
¾ cup (195g) bottled tomato sauce
9½ ounces (300g) bacon slices, chopped finely
1 cup (100g) pizza cheese
8 ounces (250g) cherry truss tomatoes
2 eggs, beaten lightly

1 Preheat oven to 475°F. Oil two oven or pizza trays; place in heated oven for 5 minutes.
2 Place pizza bases on trays, spread with sauce; top with bacon, sprinkle with cheese, top with small bunches of tomatoes.
3 Bake pizzas 10 minutes; remove from oven. Drizzle with egg. Bake pizzas about 5 minutes or until bases are browned and crisp.

prep + cook time 25 minutes **serves** 4
nutritional count per serving 19.7g total fat (7.4g saturated fat); 594 cal; 63.8g carbohydrate; 36.8g protein; 6.1g fiber

If you prefer the egg cooked through, break the yolk when adding the egg to the pizza and spread over the cheese with a spatula.

burger-style with the lot pizza

1 tablespoon olive oil

9½ ounces (300g) ground beef

2 tablespoons ketchup

2 12-inch round pizza bases (440g)

¾ cup (195g) bottled tomato sauce

⅔ cup (70g) pizza cheese

1 small red onion (100g), sliced thinly

2 eggs

2 tablespoons coarsely chopped fresh
  flat-leaf parsley

1 Preheat oven to 475°F. Oil two oven or pizza trays; place in heated oven.

2 Heat oil in large frying pan; cook beef, stirring, about 3 minutes or until browned. Stir in tomato sauce; remove from heat, season.

3 Place pizza bases on trays; spread with pasta sauce. Top with cheese, beef mixture and onion.

4 Bake pizzas 10 minutes; remove from oven. Carefully crack eggs onto pizzas. Bake pizzas about 5 minutes or until egg is cooked and bases are browned and crisp. Sprinkle with parsley.

prep + cook time 35 minutes **serves** 4
nutritional count per serving 21.6g total fat (7.3g saturated fat); 606 cal; 65.7g carbohydrate; 34.4g protein; 5.9g fiber

eggplant and prosciutto pizza

2 cloves garlic, crushed

1 tablespoon olive oil

2 8-inch x 12-inch rectangular pizza bases (440g)

11 ounces (350g) drained char-grilled eggplant

6½ ounces (200g) bocconcini cheese, torn

8 ounces (250g) cherry tomatoes

3 ounces (100g) thinly sliced prosciutto,
   chopped coarsely

1½ ounces (40g) arugula

2 teaspoons olive oil, extra

1 teaspoon balsamic vinegar

1 Preheat oven to 475°F. Oil oven trays; place in heated oven.

2 Combine garlic and oil in small bowl. Place pizza bases on trays; brush with oil mixture. Top with eggplant, cheese and tomatoes; season.

3 Bake pizzas about 15 minutes or until bases are browned and crisp. Serve topped with prosciutto and arugula. Drizzle with combined extra oil and vinegar.

prep + cook time 30 minutes **serves** 4
nutritional count per serving 22.2g total fat (7.3g saturated fat); 677 cal; 84.9g carbohydrate; 28.8g protein; 10.5g fiber

If you can't buy char-grilled zucchini, you can make your own. Use a mandoline or vegetable peeler to thinly slice one large zucchini lengthways, then cook the slices on a heated oiled grill plate until lightly browned and tender.

ratatouille pizzas

2 10-inch round pizza bases (300g)
⅓ cup (85g) bottled tomato sauce
2 tablespoons coarsely chopped fresh basil
5 ounces (160g) each drained char-grilled
    eggplant, zucchini and bell pepper
3 ounces (100g) bocconcini cheese, halved

prep + cook time 35 minutes **serves** 4
nutritional count per serving 7.4g total fat
(2.9g saturated fat); 316 cal; 45.5g carbohydrate;
13.4g protein; 6.2g fiber

1 Preheat oven to 475°F. Oil oven or pizza trays; place in heated oven for 5 minutes.
2 Place pizza bases on trays, spread with sauce; sprinkle with basil. Top with eggplant, zucchini, bell pepper and cheese; season.
3 Bake pizzas about 15 minutes or until bases are browned and crisp.

We used an arrabbiata-style pasta sauce for this recipe; it is a tomato-based pasta sauce that has been infused with chili, onion, garlic and sometimes pancetta. You can use any bottled tomato sauce you like.

pepperoni pizza

2 12-inch round pizza bases (440g)
1 cup (260g) bottled arrabbiata pasta sauce
1½ cups (150g) pizza cheese
4 ounces (125g) thinly sliced pepperoni
1 small red bell pepper (150g), sliced thinly

prep + cook time 30 minutes **serves** 4
nutritional count per serving 24.5g total fat (9.9g saturated fat); 610 cal; 65g carbohydrate; 29.4g protein; 5.9g fiber

1 Preheat oven to 475°F. Oil two oven or pizza trays; place in heated oven for 5 minutes.
2 Place pizza bases on trays, spread with sauce; sprinkle with ½ cup of the cheese. Top with pepperoni and red bell pepper; sprinkle with remaining cheese, season.
3 Bake pizzas about 15 minutes or until bases are browned and crisp.

Pre-made salsa verde is available from large supermarkets and delis; you will find it near the pesto in the condiment aisle.

tuna with salsa verde pizza

5 ounces (155g) cream cheese, softened
⅓ cup (90g) salsa verde
2 12-inch round pizza bases (440g)
6½ ounces (200g) grape tomatoes, halved
12 ounces (375g) canned tuna slices in oil, drained
½ small red onion (50g), sliced thinly

1 Preheat oven to 475°F. Oil two oven or pizza trays; place in heated oven.
2 Combine cheese and 2 tablespoons of the salsa in small bowl. Place pizza bases on trays, spread with cheese mixture. Top with tomato; season.
3 Bake pizzas about 15 minutes or until bases are browned and crisp. Serve pizzas topped with tuna and onion; drizzle with remaining salsa.

prep + cook time 35 minutes **serves** 4
nutritional count per serving 36.4g total fat (12.4g saturated fat); 720 cal; 61.3g carbohydrate; 34.3g protein; 5.5g fiber

barbecue chicken pizza

2 12-inch round pizza bases (440g)
⅓ cup (95g) barbecue sauce
1½ cups (200g) shredded barbecued chicken
1 small red onion (100g), sliced thinly
1 flat mushroom (80g) sliced thinly
½ cup (50g) pizza cheese
2 tablespoons fresh flat-leaf parsley leaves

1 Preheat oven to 475°F. Oil two oven or pizza trays; place trays in heated oven.
2 Place pizza bases on trays, spread with sauce; top with chicken, onion and mushroom. Sprinkle with cheese; season.
3 Bake pizzas about 15 minutes or until bases are browned and crisp. Sprinkle with parsley.

prep + cook time 35 minutes **serves** 4
nutritional count per serving 11.5g total fat (3.6g saturated fat); 511 cal; 70.5g carbohydrate; 28.5g protein; 5.7g fiber

If you can't buy char-grilled zucchini, you can make your own. Use a mandoline or vegetable peeler to thinly slice one large zucchini lengthways, then cook the slices on a heated oiled grill plate until browned lightly and tender.

zucchini and feta pizza

2 8-inch x 12-inch rectangular pizza bases (440g)
2 teaspoons olive oil
9½ ounces (300g) drained char-grilled zucchini
2 ounces (60g) feta cheese, crumbled
8 bocconcini cheeses (80g), halved
2 tablespoons coarsely chopped fresh oregano

1 Preheat oven to 475°F. Oil two oven or pizza trays; place in heated oven for 5 minutes.
2 Place pizza bases on trays, brush with oil; top with zucchini, cheeses and oregano, season.
3 Bake pizzas about 15 minutes or until bases are browned and crisp.

prep + cook time 35 minutes **serves** 4
nutritional count per serving 13.3g total fat (5.2g saturated fat); 439 cal; 59.7g carbohydrate; 17g protein; 5.5g fiber

Sopressa, Italian aged salami, has a spicy, slightly sweet taste with hints of pepper and garlic. Chorizo has its origins in Spanish cuisine, and gets its smoky flavor and deep red color from smoked pimentó, more commonly known as paprika. Both meats can be quite spicy so taste the different varieties on offer at the delicatessen before making this pizza.

meat lovers' pizza

1 tablespoon olive oil
1 medium brown onion (150g), chopped finely
6½ ounces (200g) ground beef
1 clove garlic, crushed
1 cup (260g) bottled tomato sauce
2 12-inch round pizza bases (440g)
1 cup (100g) pizza cheese
6 large slices hot sopressa salami (60g), halved
1 cured chorizo sausage (170g), sliced thickly

1 Preheat oven to 475°F. Oil two oven or pizza trays; place in heated oven.
2 Heat oil in large frying pan; cook onion until softened. Add beef and garlic; cook, stirring, about 3 minutes or until beef is browned. Stir in sauce; remove from heat, season.
3 Place pizza bases on trays, spread with beef mixture, sprinkle with cheese. Top with salami and chorizo.
4 Bake pizzas about 15 minutes or until bases are browned and crisp.

prep + cook time 35 minutes **serves** 4
nutritional count per serving 37.4g total fat (13.1g saturated fat); 774 cal; 66.7g carbohydrate; 40.2g protein; 6.3g fiber

spinach and egg pizza

1 pound (500g) frozen chopped spinach, thawed
1 cup (240g) ricotta cheese
2 cloves garlic, crushed
2 8-inch x 12-inch rectangular pizza bases (440g)
⅔ cup (70g) pizza cheese
2 eggs, beaten lightly

1 Preheat oven to 475°F. Oil two oven or pizza trays; place in heated oven.
2 Drain spinach; squeeze out excess liquid. Combine spinach, ricotta and garlic in medium bowl; season.
3 Place pizza bases on trays; spread with spinach mixture. Sprinkle with pizza cheese.
4 Bake pizzas 10 minutes; remove from oven. Drizzle egg over pizzas. Bake about 5 minutes or until egg is cooked and bases are browned and crisp.

prep + cook time 35 minutes **serves** 4
nutritional count per serving 18.1g total fat (8.3g saturated fat); 542 cal; 60.1g carbohydrate; 29g protein; 11.2g fiber

All the ingredients for this pizza can be picked up from your local delicatessen, making it the ultimate in tasty convenient cooking.

pesto, artichoke and prosciutto pizza

2 12-inch round pizza bases (440g)

¼ cup (65g) basil pesto

2 medium tomatoes (300g), sliced thinly

9 ounces (280g) bottled artichoke hearts, drained, halved

6 ounces (185g) bocconcini cheese, drained, halved

3 ounces (100g) thinly sliced prosciutto, chopped coarsely

¼ cup loosely packed fresh small basil leaves

1 Preheat oven to 475°F. Oil two oven or pizza trays; place in heated oven for 5 minutes.
2 Place pizza bases on trays, spread with pesto; top with tomato, artichoke and cheese, season.
3 Bake pizzas about 15 minutes or until bases are browned and crisp. Top with prosciutto; sprinkle with basil.

prep + cook time 35 minutes **serves** 4
nutritional count per serving 19g total fat (6.6g saturated fat); 536 cal; 61.9g carbohydrate; 25.4g protein; 7.2g fiber

Squeeze artichokes before halving to remove the excess moisture.

fruit and marshmallow dessert pizzas

8 4½-inch round pizza bases (340g)
cooking-oil spray
1 small banana (130g), sliced thinly
8 ounces (250g) strawberries, quartered
2 ounces (60g) pink and white marshmallows
⅓ cup (80ml) caramel topping

1 Preheat oven to 475°F. Oil two oven or pizza trays; place in heated oven for 5 minutes.
2 Place pizza bases on trays; spray with cooking oil.
3 Bake pizzas 7 minutes; remove from oven. Top with banana, strawberries and marshmallows. Bake about 4 minutes or until bases are browned and crisp. Drizzle with caramel topping.

prep + cook time 15 minutes **makes** 8
nutritional count per pizza 1.8g total fat (0.3g saturated fat); 200 cal; 41g carbohydrate; 5.1g protein; 2.5g fiber

basic pizza dough

1½ cups (225g) bread flour or plain (all-purpose)
  flour
1 teaspoon (4g) dried yeast
1 teaspoon superfine sugar
1 teaspoon fine table salt
1 tablespoon olive oil
½ cup (125ml) warm water, approximately

1 Combine flour, yeast, sugar and salt in medium
bowl; make a well in the center. Stir in oil and enough
of the water to mix to a soft dough. Knead dough
on floured surface about 10 minutes or until smooth
and elastic.
2 Place dough in large oiled bowl, cover with plastic
wrap then tea towel; stand in a warm place about
1 hour or until dough doubles in size.
3 Punch down dough with fist. Turn dough onto
a floured surface and knead about 3 minutes or
until smooth.

prep time 20 minutes (+ standing)
makes 2 12-inch round pizza bases.

In the Basic Pizza Dough recipe there is the option
of using bread flour or plain (all-purpose) flour.
Experimenting is the only way to work out what works
best for you, but as a basic guideline you can expect
to find the following results:

• If you prefer a strong, crispy crust then bread flour is
an ideal choice. The high gluten content (about 14
percent protein) will give you a sturdy crust that will
snap when you take that first bite, and remain a nice
solid base for heavier toppings.

• Most people have plain flour in their pantry; it
will give you a pizza base somewhere in between
the two previously mentioned.

tomato pizza sauce

1 tablespoon olive oil

1 small brown onion (100g), chopped finely

2 cloves garlic, crushed

12½ ounces (400g) canned chopped tomatoes

3 medium ripe plum tomatoes (225g), chopped coarsely

2 sprigs fresh thyme

1 teaspoon superfine sugar

1 Heat oil in medium saucepan; cook onion and garlic, stirring, until onion softens.

2 Add remaining ingredients; cook, uncovered, stirring occasionally, about 10 minutes or until sauce is thick. Season to taste.

glossary

almonds flat, pointy-ended nuts with a pitted brown shell enclosing a creamy white kernel that is covered by a brown skin.
meal also known as ground almonds; nuts are powdered to a coarse flour-like texture.
slivered small lengthways-cut pieces.

anchovies, white these are simply fresh anchovies that have been marinated in a mixture of oil and vinegar, the latter being the ingredient that whitens them. Available from good delicatessens.

artichokes, globe the bud of a large plant from the thistle family. It has tough, petal-shaped leaves that, once removed, reveal the inedible prickly choke, which is then discarded. The tender artichoke heart and meaty bottom can be eaten. Artichokes are also available char-grilled and artichoke hearts are available packed in brine.

bacon slices also known as rashers of bacon, made from pork side, cured and smoked.

balsamic vinegar originally from Modena, Italy, there are now many balsamic vinegars on the market, which range in both pungency and quality depending on how long they have been aged. Quality can be determined up to a point by price; use the most expensive sparingly. Has a deep rich brown color and a sweet/sour flavor.

beet firm, round, root vegetable.

black lumpfish roe (black caviar) lumpfish are found in the northern regions of the North Pacific and North Atlantic oceans. The roe is usually dyed red or black, and is salted then canned. The eggs have a nice crunchy pop with a lightly salted flavor.

butter use salted or unsalted (sweet) butter; 4 ounces is equal to one stick butter.

butternut squash pear-shaped with golden skin, orange flesh and a sweet nutty taste.

cabanossi a processed sausage popular in Southern Europe. Made from pork and beef, and seasoned with spices and garlic. Traditionally wood smoked for its flavor.

cajun seasoning used to give an authentic USA deep-south spicy cajun flavor to food; a packaged blend of assorted herbs and spices including paprika, basil, onion, fennel, thyme, cayenne and tarragon.

calamari also known as squid; a type of mollusk. Buy squid hoods to make preparation and cooking faster.

capers the grey-green buds of a warm climate (usually Mediterranean) shrub, sold either dried and salted or pickled in a vinegar brine; tiny young ones, called baby capers, are also available. Capers, whether packed in brine or in salt, must be rinsed well before using.

bell pepper also known as pepper. They can be red, green, yellow, orange or purplish-black. Discard seeds and membranes before use.
roasted red available loose or packed in jars in oil or brine from delicatessens and supermarkets.

chicken tenderloin thin tender strip of meat lying just under the breast.

chili available in many different types and sizes. Use rubber gloves when seeding and chopping fresh chilies as they can burn your skin. Removing seeds and membranes lessens the heat level.
flakes dried, deep-red, dehydrated chili slices and whole seeds.
green any unripened chili, or those varieties that are ripe when green.
jalapeño fairly hot green chilies. Sold fresh, chopped or whole and bottled in vinegar.

chocolate hazelnut spread we use Nutella; developed during World War II when chocolate was in short supply, hazelnuts were added to extend the chocolate.

chorizo sausage of Spanish origin, made of coarsely ground pork and highly seasoned with garlic and chili. They are deeply smoked, very spicy and dry-cured. Also available raw.

cinnamon dried inner bark of the shoots of the cinnamon tree; available in stick (quill) or ground form.

cream
crème fraîche a mature, naturally fermented cream. It has a velvety texture and a slightly tangy, nutty flavor. Can boil without curdling and is used in both sweet and savoury dishes. Minimum fat content 35 percent.
light sour a thick, cultured soured cream with a 18.5 percent fat content.

cumin a spice also known as zeera or comino; has a spicy, nutty flavor.

dried currants small dried grape that looks like a tiny black raisin. Not the same as fresh currants.

eggplant purple-skinned vegetable also known as aubergine. Char-grilled eggplant is also available, packed in oil, in jars.

fennel bulb also known as anise or finocchio; a firm, white to very pale green-white, crisp, roundish vegetable about 3 to 4¾ inches in diameter. The bulb has a slightly sweet, anise flavor but the leaves have a much stronger taste. Also the name given to dried seeds having a licorice flavor.

figs vary in skin and flesh color according to type, not ripeness. When ripe, figs should be unblemished and bursting with flesh; nectar beads at the base indicate when a fig is at its best.

flour
bread is a strong flour, meaning it has a relatively high gluten content; this causes bread to rise, giving it shape and structure. It is available from most supermarkets.

plain an all-purpose flour made from wheat. Not as strong as bread flour.

ginger, ground also known as powdered ginger; used as a flavoring in cakes, pies and puddings but can't be substituted for fresh ginger.

ham made from cured and smoked boned hind pork leg.

hummus a Middle-Eastern sauce or dip made from softened dried chickpeas, garlic, lemon juice and tahini (sesame seed paste); can be purchased, ready-made, from most delicatessens and supermarkets.

lamb

backstrap the larger fillet from a row of loin chops or cutlets. May also be sold as lamb fillet instead.

shanks, french-trimmed also known as drumsticks or frenched shanks; all the gristle and narrow end of the bone is discarded then the remaining meat trimmed.

maple syrup a thin syrup distilled from the sap of the maple tree. Maple-flavored syrup or pancake syrup is not an adequate substitute for the real thing.

marshmallows soft, light, airy confectionery made from sugar, glucose, gelatin and cornstarch.

mushrooms

button small, cultivated white mushrooms with a mild flavor.

field large and meaty with an earthy taste; available as wild and cultivated mushrooms. If wild, they must be certified as non-toxic before eating.

oyster also known as abalone; grey-white mushroom shaped like a fan. Prized for their smooth texture and subtle, oyster-like, flavor.

porcini, dried the richest flavored mushrooms, also known as cèpes. Has a strong nutty flavor, so only small amounts are required for most dishes. Must be rehydrated before use.

shiitake when fresh are also known as chinese black, forest or golden oak mushrooms; although cultivated, have the earthiness and taste of wild mushrooms. Are large and meaty. When dried, they are known as donko or dried chinese mushrooms; rehydrate before use.

mussels should be bought from a fish market where there is reliably fresh fish; they must be tightly closed when bought, indicating they are alive. Before cooking, scrub the shells with a strong brush and remove the beards. Some mussels may not open after cooking; these might not have cooked as quickly as the others and need further cooking, or try carefully opening with a knife.

nuts

pecan golden-brown, rich, buttery nut.

pine nuts also known as pignoli; not in fact a nut but small, cream-colored kernels from pine cones.

pistachio pale green, delicately flavored nut inside a hard off-white shell. To peel, soak shelled nuts in boiling water for about 5 minutes; drain, then pat dry with paper towels. Rub skins with cloth to peel.

walnut encased in a grooved, light-brown shell; has a mildly sweet, and sometimes bitter, taste.

oil

olive made from ripened olives. Extra virgin and virgin are the first and second press, respectively, and are therefore considered the best, while extra light or light is diluted and refers to taste not fat levels.

peanut pressed from ground peanuts; has a high smoke point (capacity to handle high heat without burning).

sesame made from roasted, crushed, white sesame seeds.

vegetable sourced from plants.

olives

black have a richer and more mellow flavor than the green ones and are softer in texture. Sold either plain or in a piquant marinade.

green those harvested before fully ripened and are, as a rule, denser and more bitter than their black relatives.

kalamata small, sharp-tasting, brine-cured black olives.

onions

brown are interchangeable with white, however, white onions have a more pungent flesh.

green also known as scallion or, incorrectly, shallot; an immature onion picked before the bulb has formed. Has a long, bright-green, edible stalk.

red also known as spanish, red spanish or bermuda onion; a sweet-flavored, large, purple-red onion.

shallots also called french shallots, golden shallots or eschalots; small, brown-skinned, elongated members of the onion family.

spring are onions with small white bulbs and long, narrow green-leafed tops.

pancetta cured pork belly; bacon can be substituted.

paprika ground dried sweet red bell pepper; there are many types, including mild, hot, sweet and smoked.

pepperoni a spicy variety of dry salami usually made of pork or beef, and heavily seasoned with spices.

pita bread also known as lebanese bread. This wheat-flour pocket bread is sold in large, flat pieces that separate into two thin rounds. Also available in small thick pieces called pocket pita.

pizza bases pre-packaged for home-made pizzas. Come as snack or family size and thin and crispy or thick.

pizza bruschettina a par-baked pizza bread; available from most major supermarkets.

pomegranate is native to the Middle-East. A leathery-skinned, dark-red fruit about the size of an orange; is filled with hundreds of seeds, each wrapped in an edible lucent-crimson pulp with a tangy sweet-sour flavor.

popping corn is labelled as such, and is available from supermarkets. When heated, it expands from the kernel and puffs up.

preserved lemon rind a North African specialty; lemons are preserved in salt and lemon juice or water. To use, remove and discard pulp, squeeze juice from rind, rinse well, then slice rind thinly.

prosciutto cured, air-dried (unsmoked), pressed ham; usually sold thinly sliced.

quinoa (keen-wa) the seed of a leafy plant similar to spinach. Its cooking qualities are similar to rice; it has a delicate, slightly nutty taste and chewy texture. Available in most health-food stores; keep sealed in a glass jar under refrigeration as it spoils easily.

radicchio a member of the chicory family. Has dark burgundy leaves and a strong bitter flavor.

ras el hanout a classic spice blend used in Moroccan cooking. The name means 'top of the shop'; it is the very best spice blend that a spice merchant has to offer.

saffron available in strands (threads) or ground form; imparts a yellow-orange color to food once infused. Quality varies greatly; the best is the most expensive spice in the world. Should be stored in the freezer.

salami cured (air-dried) sausages heavily seasoned with garlic and spices.

salmon roe salmon eggs that have been cured. Generally less expensive than caviar, although it lacks the complex and rich flavor associated with caviar products.

salt
cooking is coarser than table salt, but not as large-flaked as sea salt: it is sold packaged in bags in most supermarkets.
flakes reminiscent of snowflakes. Sea water is evaporated producing a salt brine that is fed into an open evaporating pan. The brine is then slowly heated until delicate pyramid-shaped crystals of salt appear.
table this is the common salt normally found on every table. It is a finely ground, refined rock salt with some additives to keep it free-flowing. Most table salt is available either plain or iodized.

sauces
arrabbiata a hot and spicy sauce made with tomatoes and red chili.
barbecue a spicy, tomato-based sauce used to marinate or as a condiment.
ketchup also known as catsup; a flavored condiment made from tomatoes, vinegar and spices.
pizza a tomato sauce for spreading over pizza bases. Usually found next to the tomato paste in supermarkets.
satay traditional Indonesian/Malaysian spicy peanut sauce served with grilled meat skewers. Make your own or buy one of the many packaged versions easily obtained from supermarkets or specialty Asian food stores.
tomato made from puréed tomatoes. Sold in jars; can be smooth or chunky.

sausages, italian style a coarse pork sausage, generally sold in plump links. Italian sausage is usually flavored with garlic and fennel seeds or anise seeds. It comes in two styles – hot (flavored with thai red chili) and sweet (without the added heat). It must be well cooked before serving.

semolina made from durum wheat milled into various textured granules, all of these finer than flour.

shrimp varieties include sydney harbour, king, royal red, school and tiger. Can be bought uncooked (green) or cooked, with or without shells.

spinach is also known as english spinach and, incorrectly, silver beet. Its thick, soft oval leaves and green stems are both edible. Baby spinach is also available.

stock cans, bottles, tetra packs, cubes, powder or concentrated liquid can be used. As a guide, 1 teaspoon of stock powder or 1 small crumbled stock cube mixed with 1 cup water will give a fairly strong stock.

sugar
brown a soft, finely granulated sugar retaining molasses for its characteristic color and flavor.
confectioners' sugar also known as powdered sugar; granulated sugar crushed with a little cornstarch.
palm also known as nam tan pip, jaggery, jawa or gula melaka; made from the sap of the sugar palm tree. Light brown to black in color and usually sold in rock-hard cakes; the sugar of choice in Indian and most South-East Asian cooking. Substitute it with brown sugar if unavailable.
superfine also known as finely granulated table sugar.
white a coarse, granulated table sugar, also known as crystal sugar.

sumac purple-red, astringent spice ground from shrub berries flourish wild in the Mediterranean; adds a tart, lemony flavor. Available from Middle-Eastern food stores and some larger supermarkets.

taco seasoning mix found in most supermarkets; is meant to duplicate the taste of a Mexican sauce made from oregano, cumin, chilies and other spices.

taramasalata a thick dip made from fish roe, olive oil, seasonings and breadcrumbs. Available from the refrigerated section of supermarkets.

tomato
cherry also known as tiny tim or tom thumb tomatoes; small and round.
grape about the size of a grape; they can be oblong, pear or grape-shaped.
pesto, sun-dried a thick paste made from sun-dried tomatoes, oil, vinegar and herbs.
plum also called egg or roma, smallish, oval-shaped tomatoes much used in Italian cooking.

tortillas thin, round unleavened bread originating in Mexico. Can be made from either corn or wheat flour.

vanilla
bean dried long, thin pod from a tropical golden orchid grown in Central and South America and Tahiti; the tiny black seeds inside the bean impart a luscious vanilla flavor in baking and desserts.
extract made by pulping chopped vanilla beans with a mixture of alcohol and water. This gives a very strong solution, and only a couple of drops are needed for flavor.

yeast a ¼oz (7g) sachet of dried yeast (2 teaspoons) is equal to ½oz (15g) compressed yeast if substituting one for the other.

yogurt we used plain, unflavored yogurt, unless otherwise specified.
greek-style often made from sheep's milk; its thick, smooth consistency, almost like whipped cream, is achieved by draining off the milk liquids.

zucchini also known as courgette; small, pale- or dark-green, yellow or white vegetable belonging to the squash family. Harvested when young, its edible flowers can be stuffed then deep-fried or oven-baked to make a delicious appetizer.

conversion chart

measures

One metric measuring cup holds approximately 250ml; one metric tablespoon holds 20ml; one metric teaspoon holds 5ml.

The difference between one country's measuring cups and another's is within a two- or three-teaspoon variance, and will not affect your cooking results. North America, New Zealand and the United Kingdom use a 15ml tablespoon.

All cup and spoon measurements are level. The most accurate way of measuring dry ingredients is to weigh them. When measuring liquids, use a clear glass or plastic jug with the metric markings.

We use large eggs with an average weight of 2oz/60g.

dry measures

METRIC	IMPERIAL
15g	½oz
30g	1oz
60g	2oz
90g	3oz
125g	4oz (¼lb)
155g	5oz
185g	6oz
220g	7oz
250g	8oz (½lb)
280g	9oz
315g	10oz
345g	11oz
375g	12oz (¾lb)
410g	13oz
440g	14oz
470g	15oz
500g	16oz (1lb)
750g	24oz (1½lb)
1kg	32oz (2lb)

liquid measures

METRIC	IMPERIAL
30ml	1 fluid oz
60ml	2 fluid oz
100ml	3 fluid oz
125ml	4 fluid oz
150ml	5 fluid oz
190ml	6 fluid oz
250ml	8 fluid oz
300ml	10 fluid oz
500ml	16 fluid oz
600ml	20 fluid oz
1000ml (1 litre)	1¾ pints

length measures

3mm	⅛in
6mm	¼in
1cm	½in
2cm	¾in
2.5cm	1in
5cm	2in
6cm	2½in
8cm	3in
10cm	4in
13cm	5in
15cm	6in
18cm	7in
20cm	8in
22cm	9in
25cm	10in
28cm	11in
30cm	12in (1ft)

index

METRO BOOKS
New York

An Imprint of Sterling Publishing
387 Park Avenue South
New York, NY 10016

METRO BOOKS and the distinctive Metro Books logo
are trademarks of Sterling Publishing Co., Inc.

© 2013 by ACP Magazines Ltd.

This 2013 edition published by Metro Books by arrangement with ACP Magazines Ltd.

ISBN 978-1-4351-4529-0

For information about custom editions, special sales, and premium and corporate purchases,
please contact Sterling Special Sales at 800-805-5489 or specialsales@sterlingpublishing.com.

Manufactured in China

2 4 6 8 10 9 7 5 3 1

www.sterlingpublishing.com